Restaurant Business Plan

The Complete Practical Format

Allen Mbengeranwa

Executive Summary

Business Name: Papa Bengie's™

Business Address: Menai, Bangor

Personal Address: Ynys Mon, Bangor

Projected first year turnover: £159,000.00

Funding requirements: £450,000.00. To purchase property, £375,000.00; fixed assets and improvements, £10,498.06; equipment purchases, £32,690.09; start-up costs, £10,540.00 and capital requirements of £21,271.05.

Other requirements: To create a management team. The business will need a Business mentor or non-executive director to assist in creating a long term business model with potential to expand.

Business Idea: Quick Service Restaurant targeted at the mid-market serving handmade grilled Beef burgers; boned grilled chicken quarters with choice of sauce from six, seared tuna steaks with anchovy and orange butter; King prawn brochettes; Veg mince burgers and a range of accompaniments including fries, Papa's flavoured rice, coleslaw and a selection of starters. The business model will also feature free refills for post-mix drinks to dining customers and a takeaway option. The restaurant also features a corkage facility that will charge £2.00 for customers to bring their own wine. These facilities will form part of the Unique Selling Propositions that will give us a competitive advantage in the local market.

Market Addressed: Mid-market quick service restaurant serving lunch and evening meals focusing on healthy double grilled Beef burgers and Grilled chicken to order.

Location: 208 High Street, Bangor. The premises occupy a prime retail location within the pedestrians section of the High Street, close to many multiples including W H Smith, Argos, Debenhams, Yates, Fat cat café bar, a J D Weatherspoon's. Bangor is the principal shopping centre of the county of Gwynedd and Anglesey and thus enjoys a wide

Allen Mbengeranwa

catchment area in addition to being a university city. There are also no less than four public car parks, including National Car parks.

Staffing Levels: One full time assistant manager forming part of up to 7 part time employees, variable. The experienced assistant manager will also form part of the core management team.

Business status: Start-Up

Responsibilities: Start-up activities and part of daily management team.

Keys to Success: Creating a unique, innovative mid-scale service and atmosphere that will differentiate us from the competition.
Constantly meeting Papa Bengie's ™primary goal to serve the best value grilled meals to enhance customer experience 100% of the time.
Operating an efficient business model that includes tight control on all systems designed for Papa Bengie's

Hiring the best people available, training, motivating and encouraging the team and thereby retaining the friendliest, most efficient team of staff possible.

Long-term view: The business concept is sound and will be developed into a quick service restaurant brand. The possibility of opening other restaurants will be considered along with the necessary management team, financial and organisational structure necessary to make the expansion a success. This view is taken into consideration in year three. The main objective is to repay the current debt and offer a return to the constituents.

Exit routes: For the initial funding, there is a payment of interest and loan capital over a five year period. There is an option, to recoup the funding earlier as the majority of the finance is needed to fund the purchase of property. As the value of the premises will increase with the development, a commercial re-mortgage will return capital to the initial sources of finance.

Allen Mbengeranwa

Executive Summary 2

Table of Figures...7

Background 8

Products/service and operations 9

Resource plan..20

Operating and control systems....................................22

The Market & Marketing...32

The Competition 46

Pricing...47

Premises..65

Capital Expenditure 67

Legal Aspects 70

Financial Information 71

Financial Deal 78

Appendix 86

    Administration Costs...86

    Equipment Inventory..87

    Establishment/Property Costs 88

    Finance Costs Year One..89

    Profit and Loss Year One Summary Sheet.......................90

    Profit and Loss Year Two Summary Sheet.......................91

    Opening Stock Format 92

    Pre Trading Cash Flow Forecast 93

    Sales Costs..94

    Cash-flow forecasts – Year One......................................95

    Cash-flow forecasts – Year Two......................................96

Table of Figures

Figure 1 Operating and Control Systems Model.................22
Figure 2 Sales Management System........................25
Figure 3 Market Research.............................33
Figure 4 Market Demographics 35
Figure 5 Direct competition Research 46
Figure 6 Service Creation Model........................59
Figure 7 Premises 66
Figure 8 Equipment Required..........................67
Figure 9 Start Up Costs 68
Figure 10 Staffing Requirements 68
Figure 11 Break even calculation.......................72
Figure 12 Sales Forcast 73
Figure 13 Cash Flow Forecast 74
Figure 14 Financial Assumptions 78
Figure 15 Financing Requirements 79
Figure 16 Timetable/Milestones.......................81
Figure 17 Balance Sheet 83
Figure 18 Pro Forma Profit and Loss Statement..........85

Allen Mbengeranwa

Background

1.0 Management team

The business model requires a business mentor with experience in the restaurant and retail industry. This will assist the business model and possible expansion plans as the business grows. At a later stage, the business will require non-executive directors that will assist in expanding the business model.

At present, the management team comprises of The Owner, a graduate of accounting and finance from the University of Wales, Bangor. Having undergone training with various business support agencies from 2001 up to the present day. .

The management team also includes The Owners Partner, who has worked for The Private Clinic, in Harley Street and Sainsbury's finance department in Streatham, London.

There are also plans to recruit an assistant manager with experience in the hotel and catering industry. The main functions of this position entail maintaining the front-end operations of the day to day running of the restaurant. This mostly includes customer service assistance and personnel management.

Products/service and operations

2.0 Product/Service description

The product plan

Within the restaurant industry, the service often becomes the product. We aim to create a strong brand by linking the service closely with the food. The product may be the food, which is tangible, but the service will also form a large part of the business concept. We aim to serve handmade grilled hamburgers and grilled, boneless chicken quarters as our main menu items.

The Papa Bengie's ™concept will centre on grilled food. There is a choice of four beef burgers and one Welsh lamb burger for the red meat grills and boned chicken, tuna and king prawns for the 'white' meat grills. There are also vegetarian items, including Veg mince burgers on the menu. The concept also has a fresh salad made from hearts of romaine with a choice of sauce.

The grilled chicken concept centres on allowing the customers to choose the sauce they want to accompany their boned, grilled quarter chicken. There is a choice of 6 different sauces to choose from when ordering. This offers customers variety and different flavours to experience with us. The range of sauces reflects the modern eating habits and growing international culture.

1. Sun dried tomato and herb
2. Thai green curry sauce
3. Caribbean spices
4. Sweet hickory barbeque sauce

Allen Mbengeranwa

5. Red pepper and olive sauce
6. Vietnamese sweet chilli sauce

Papa Bengie's ™serves boned grilled chicken quarters to ensure fuller flavour of the meat

Boning the meat, with the breast quarter looking like a French trimmed breast allows us to cook the chicken in less than 2 minutes on our double grills. The idea of using double grills is not new. This technique was perfected by McDonalds Restaurants and allowes hamburger patties to be cooked in record time and in high volumes. This method has not been introduced to chicken Quick service restaurants because of the presents of the bones.

Removing the bones allows chicken to be cooked faster and to order reducing the need to waste unsold cooked meat. Some operators may deep fry the chicken in the morning and hot-hold for long periods resulting in a reduction in the temperature of the meat plus the fats and oils. This results in the oil becoming thicker as the temperature reduces producing a piece of meat that is laden with natural and oily fats. Papa Bengie's ™boned and grilled quarters are grilled to order which reduces the natural fat content of the meat as it drains away during cooking.

Chicken Burgers

Papa Bengie's ™will also serve grilled chicken burgers. The fillet will come from the quarter chicken breast reducing the need to order separately. This also ensures that our chicken burgers are larger than ordinary breast that have had the chicken breast 'oyster' removed.

The Grilled Chicken Sandwiches are:
1. Papa's Grilled Chicken - butterfly-cut grilled chicken breast, shredded lettuce, fresh tomato, red onion, Papa's Mayo in a sesame seed bun
2. Papa's Mediterranean Chicken – butterfly-cut grilled chicken breast, bacon shredded lettuce, red onion, sliced tomato, sun dried tomato and herb in a sesame seed bun

3. Papa's Grilled Chicken in Pita - butterfly-cut grilled chicken breast, shredded lettuce, fresh tomato, red onion, Papa's Mayo in a sesame seed bun
4. Double papa's grilled chicken sandwich

Beef Burgers
Papa Bengie's ™beef burgers come in only four varieties and the same size. This means that we reduce the number of menu items and ingredients resulting in a more efficient back-of-house operation. This reduces the strain on prep staff and management systems used.

The types of beef burgers are:
1. Beef Burger with fresh lettuce, tomato, Papa Bengie's ™mayonnaise, English mustard, pickles, fresh onion and Papa Bengie's ™beef burger all in a sesame seed bun
2. Bleu Cheese Burger – Papa Bengie's ™beef burger, fresh shredded lettuce, tomato, bleu cheese crumbles, pepper sauce, onions, bleu cheese dressing in a sesame seed bun
3. BBQ Ranch burger – Papa Bengie's ™beef burger, fresh shredded lettuce, tomato, onions, bacon, BBQ sauce and ranch dressing

Allen Mbengeranwa

4. The Bacon Burger – Papa Bengie's ™beef burger, fresh shredded lettuce, tomato, onions, bacon, pickle and papa's mayo.

Grilled Fish

Papa Bengie's ™will also offer two fish meals. In keeping with the grilled food concept, Papa Bengie's ™will serve Premium Tuna steaks and grilled King Prawn Brochettes. This adds depth to the menu and allows us to offer a wider range of meals that may appeal to group dinners. All the fish will be offered on a bed of Papa's spicy rice.

Papa's Grilled fish:
1. Seared premium tuna streak with Papa's Anchovy and Orange butter
2. Two grilled king prawn brochettes with choice of Papa's sauce

Vegetarian
1. Veggie burger with shredded lettuce, fresh tomato, red onion dressed with honey and mustard
2. Pita veggie burger with shredded lettuce, fresh tomato, red onion dressed with honey and mustard

Salads
Papa's salad
1. Hearts of Romaine, croutons, anchovies, Parmesan shavings, choice of sauce:
    Ranch dressing
    Honey and mustard
    Bleu cheese dressing

2. Papa's salad with grilled chicken

Starters
1. BBQ chicken wings

2. Breaded mushrooms with choice of sauce

3. Warm pita bread with salsa

Accompaniments
These will be offered as choices to customers and form part of the meal combinations and deals:
1. French fries
2. Papa's rice
3. Coleslaw

Drinks
We will have a post mix system that will allow us to charge one price and offer free refills for drinks. This is a popular incentive and is used by Pizza Hut and Nandos. The worldwide success of Nandos and the parent company of Pizza Hut illustrate that this is a system that is successful and a good incentive for customers.

We will also offer other drinks:
Bottled drinks
1. Mineral water
2. Orange juice
3. Apple Juice
4. Coca cola
5. Raspberry and cranberry

Allen Mbengeranwa

Unique Selling Proposition

We aim to be service orientated and deliver quality experiences for our diners. We are going to have a sustained marketing campaign that is designed to engage potential and current diners outside the restaurant. We will also offer student discounts and on-duty emergency services discount. These campaigns are designed to generate sales and increase foot-flow into our restaurant.

Grilled, fresh food. It is said that fresh food is best for flavour and quality. That's what we will offer our diners by cooking their food to order.

Grilling also allows us to offer healthier food for customers as the grills will reduce the natural fat in the food. This will be highly attractive to our health and non-health conscious dinners. The customers will be able to add this health aspect of our food to their decision making when evaluating their motivators to eat out.

Aesthetic appeal. Our grills will ensure that food is cooked thoroughly and the markings created by our grill will ensure that the food looks very appetising and pleasant to the eye. It will also add to the presentation of our food and add to the delight of our customers.

Flavour Factor. Or ability to offer 6 sauces and 4 beef burger tastes means that the customers can choose a sauce to suit their tastes and moods. This is an important factor when customers are considering were to dine, the availability of choice. The seared tuna with Anchovy and orange butter will also be flavourful and aesthetically pleasing.

Diverse menu. We will offer beef burgers, chicken meals, fish dishes, vegetarian choices and fresh salads to allow a single group of diners to meet their individual needs. Diversity will also increase the level of repeat custom as more choices are available.

Bottomless soft drinks. These will be the only bottomless soft drinks available in Bangor. Everyone loves a 'freebie'.

Quick service. Papa Bengie's ™business model allows for us to serve customers quickly because of the designed preparation methods and simple menu. Allowing customers to proceed to the counter when they are ready to order means that we will serve the entire meal together, quickly. This will also reduce dining times and increase the availability of tables.

Consistency. The business model ensures that all the sauces and other food items are of the same taste, texture, quality, smell and appearance at all times. This means that customers will expect the same service and know exactly what they are getting. The other effect of this is the trust that will be developed by customers always knowing what to expect.

Corkage. We also aim to offer corkage of £2. This means that the customers can have a bottle of wine with their meal costing them £5, including our corkage fee. This means that, from an operational perspective, we will be having only a 50% mark up on

---

Allen Mbengeranwa

wine we don't stock.   This model has been known to attract customers, especially students, when cash is tight.

The corkage concept allows us to participate in the evening dining market where legally entitled adults can have a romantic meal with their choice of drink.
This will offer us a unique position in the market as we will not have a liquor licence but allow our diners to create their own ambience and generate revenue for us. We will be receiving £2.00 per bottle.

We will also have a mix of fresh ingredients to garnish our food to create an exciting presentation.   Our coleslaw will be laced with parsley and the Hearts of romaine salad served with Anchovy.

The current stage of development

At present, a suitable location has been found in the right location for the business.   The business plan has been completed and the business model is seeking funding to secure the premises.

The business concept and plans are complete and await financing.

The food and drink will be ordered at the last minute as they may be delivered the following day. Suppliers have already been contacted and preliminary arrangements made.

The time estimated from receiving funding and starting the business is three months.

Window of opportunity

The opportunity is not perpetual as the idea property is still on the market and may be acquired by someone else. It is therefore of paramount importance that the site be secured immediately. There is no available substitutable site in the market. The location is ideally placed in the 'entertainment' end of the high street where there rarely is an opportunity to enter the market. It is imperative that action is taken at once.

Capital, Labour, Material Proportions

The initial stages of the business model are capital intensive. This is because of the purchases and converting the premises into the desired use. A majority of the start-up costs are for fixed assets with a vital proportion going to marketing and sales generating activities.

Labour.

There will be active recruitment for an experienced assistant manager to be responsible for front end operations. We will use the local jobcentre, local paper and recruitment agents, for example, Atebion based in Bangor, to recruit staff

The business model is designed to use part time labour. This reduces the commitment to staff. The nature of the model means that no professional chef is required and therefore, the costs will be considerably lower.

Using part time staff accords the business model flexibility, especially at the beginning of the business.

The assistant manager will be working on full time hours with days off.

Material.
In this instance, the food will be purchased on a rolling basis. The level of sales will determine the amount of material ordered. This vital variable cost will be monitored constantly. This will not be difficult as there are few menu lines.

This task will be helped by the use of the quality accounting and restaurant software chosen for the operations.

Government approvals
The property currently does not have the necessary consents to operate as a restaurant. There are plans to apply for A3 consent.

The premises will be available to the local environmental health department for inspection although no licences are needed at this time.

The business model does not need a liquor licence.

Potential liabilities
As a food serving establishment to members of the public, there is need for a public, product and employers liability insurance. There will also be an insurance arrangement for the motor vehicle.

Insurances

There will be the mandatory public, product liability insurance and employers' liability insurance. There are insurance packages that are available and will cost £1,000.00 per year that are comprehensive to the restaurant industry. The insurance will also include a business continuity element to cover any disruptions

Allen Mbengeranwa

Resource plan

The business is that of a restaurant. We will serve grilled beef burgers, grilled chicken, grilled fish, and salads plus drink in a comfortable and pleasant environment. The food will consist of a selection of meal combinations of main dishes accompanied by select starters and side dishes.

Equipment needed
This includes the grills and refrigerators and server-ware.

A complete inventory list including quantities and cost price is included in the Appendix. The majority of this equipment is available with the lease.

Stock levels:
The initial stock levels are to be determined by the meals and beverages that we will offer. We will order the minimum number of each stock item at the launch. This is in order to avoid having a large stock inventory where some meals may be difficult to sell. The numbers are made up of the minimum order cases of the suppliers. Effective monitoring of this will highlight the popular meals and where we should push the high margin meals to customers.

The Papa Bengie's ™Anchovy and Orange butter will be made to a secret recipe.

Regular stock take and daily sales checks will highlight what needs to be ordered for next day delivery. This will allow us to not only measure daily stock levels, but also to provide vital information towards the financial health of the business. This activity will be easy to undertake as there are few menu items and any discrepancies will be highlighted early on.

The stock will be obtained from leading suppliers within the industry. They are the largest suppliers and therefore, offer the security of stock availability and quality.

Staff will be recruited from the local area with an advert placed at the local job-centre for free. This will be highly effective as the level of competence required in staff is best suited to this form of local advertising.

For the inventory, we will be unable to lease any equipment the result being outright purchase. We will also have to pay cash for the ingredients and supplies. This is because new restaurants are unable to raise lines of credit with suppliers.

All staff will be on part time contracts on a temporary basis for a probation period of three months. A performance and business review will then highlight whether a permanent contract be granted or not.

We will have a next day delivery lead time. This is standard in catering and the suppliers achieve this at all times. This means that we will be able to order stock online at the end of business and have it ready for the next trading day in time for opening.

Allen Mbengeranwa

Operating and control systems

This is the model that will be used to monitor and control the venture.

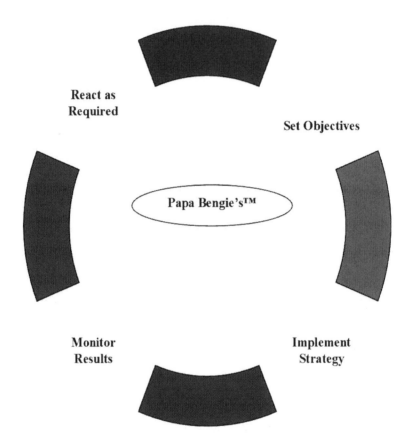

Figure 1 Operating and Control Systems Model

FOOD MANUAL

I have created a food manual for the Papa Bengie's ™restaurant concept. This will be used to ensure consistency of quality in the service delivery. The food manual created will also be useful when there is a change of staff.

1. The specifications for the raw ingredients, cook times and temperature for each item and the size of each portion.
2. Preparation procedures
3. Holding times and temperatures.
4. Procedures for handling left-overs
5. Food storage procedures
6. Food safety procedures
7. Food cost for each portion and suggested price
8. A nutritional analysis of each menu item or dish.

Employee theft

There are three main types of employee theft that will be mentioned in the Papa Bengie's ™concept:
1. under-ringing of sales and tearing up of food tickets
2. food theft or taking home supplies
3. Leaving and coming in at a later time to clock out.

The operations manual contains details of how to detect employee theft through:
- ❖ signals from personal behaviour
- ❖ signals from employee behaviour
  - ❖ signals from customers and outsiders

Allen Mbengeranwa

Internal security measures

These are some of the measures to be used to control employee theft:

1. Provide information on internal security measures
2. Surveillance
3. Inventory checks
4. Information on the likelihood and consequences of being caught stealing.
5. CASH and till control measures

This information is highly sensitive, it has therefore, not been included in the open business plan of Papa Bengie's.

Selling and sales management

The advertising and marketing activities will be used to drive sales. We will augment this by offering a great service and having a constant message in the local area.

Our sales and marketing controls will seek to monitor the effectiveness of plans. We will monitor the results of various activities such as Local Area Businesses Marketing (LABM). This is a first for a restaurant in the area and will further enhance our reputation and drive sales.

This is an extract from the system that will be used to monitor the sales:

Week Beginning	No. of enquiries received – emial Phone/foot flow	No. of leaflets received/sent	LABM	Blue lights	Cost of weeks activities	Estimate of sales worth of weeks activities

Figure 2 Sales Management System

The information will be entered onto the system from a telephone sheet and receipts. This is a management function.

Employee related systems

There will be files created for each employee. These will include:
1. Contract of employment
2. Pay records and details including PAYE and National Insurance
3. Job description pack and completed application form
4. Interview responses and health questionnaires
5. Training and development plan and records
6. Evaluations and disciplinary

Allen Mbengeranwa

Customers and marketing systems

1. Complaints procedure and reporting
2. Discounts and offers systems that allow for easy monitoring and evaluation.
3. Refunds procedure.

Premises and Assets Administration

There will be an assets register which will include:
1. Equipment type, supplier and purchase costs
2. Warranty details and maintenance records/check
3. Cleaning schedule
4. Insurance details
5. Operating manual and training guide.
6. Copy of lease and physical building items

Legal and insurance issues

This section will include files on:
1. insurance policies and cover
2. lease details contract and solicitors affairs
3. details of any warrantees and liability issues
4. council affairs such as planning and building control
5. environmental health correspondence and requirements
6. licensing

Suppliers

This will include:
1. list of products and services
2. ordering procedure and lead times
3. any warrantees and liabilities
4. conditions of sale
5. price checks and comparisons

Financial Administrative policies, procedures and controls

There will be systems for:
1. H M Customs and revenue
   - ❖ PAYE and National Insurance
   - ❖ VAT records and payments
   - ❖ Business tax
2. Financial controls
   - ❖ daily and weekly cash reporting
   - ❖ weekly profit and loss reporting
   - ❖ quarterly fixed assets report
   - ❖ monitoring of daily stock and cash
   - ❖ product costs and profitability
   - ❖ monthly balance sheet
   - ❖ stock control

Allen Mbengeranwa

The role of IT in delivering controls

The aim is to use a computer to monitor all the systems. The following items will be needed:

1. Internet enabled computer system with windows operating system
2. Sage ONE accounting software
3. Sage payroll bureau software
4. Restaurant software with reservations, stock control, point of sale and chip & pin
5. Scanner
6. Colour printer
7. Hand held personal digital assistants for floor management and operations.

The IT infrastructure is designed to increase the level of control in the business model. It will also lead to reduced loss of paper and more effective monitoring of restaurant tables and availability.

Administration infrastructure

The following will be necessary to maintain and operate the control systems:
1. Office desk and chair
2. Large secure filling unit
3. Notice board

Contingency plans

Sales projections
The sales are based on the lower end of the market research assumptions. There is capacity to cater for an increase in sales of 100%. In the event that this does happen, the booking system will be adhered to as a queuing system.

If the sales are less than expected, there will be a drive to increase advertising and marketing. We will speed up the process of developing the business to increase the revenue streams and thus total revenue. The facilities for take away and delivery will be improved and the business plans created. There are intentions to present a business plan for these additional revenue streams 6 months after opening.

At the projected level of sales, there is a fall-back position as the waste will be lower because some of the menu items are frozen. There are plans to offer meal deals from £4.90 during all hours. This will be used to drive sales and increase awareness of the restaurant generating 'peer-to-peer' marketing that may lead to an increase in evening diners.

In order to cover the low sales while there is a marketing campaign to increase sales. Reduced sales will be met with changing the staff rota to cater for the busy periods and reduce to staffing levels to a minimum. This reduction in wage costs will enable to business to meet its payments on the loan capital and interest.

Allen Mbengeranwa

The business may develop to offer catering to business and households to provide platters, canapés and snacks. This will be pushed with a business plan and implemented to ease the pressure on the restaurant.

The business model is such that there staff hours of work can be cut during quiet periods. This will be done if the sales prove to be less than anticipated while the marketing and advertising is highlighted.

Supply deficiencies
There are a number of suppliers who will offer the same products as our chosen supplier. We will contact another company for the menu items. As some items will be frozen, we will be able to push the food available that night till the next day's delivery. There are no major problems associated with supply. We are also able to sauce ingredients from local supermarkets, wholesalers and independent stores.

Product liability problems arise
As our food will be from established suppliers, we will seek to indemnify ourselves from any liabilities by pursuing suppliers as soon as any issues are identified. All foodstuffs will be sourced from recognised suppliers where every product is traceable. There is also an insurance policy that will cover the usual liabilities associated with restaurants.

For customers, we will also replace any unsatisfactory items served. The business model allows for the meals to be checked during preparation before serving customers.

Personnel problems

The business model requires low staffing levels and therefore, any issues that arise may be attended to quickly and efficiently. In the event of an employee having to leave, there is capacity for the business to continue operating with one member of staff while recruitment is taking place. It will be explained to customers that there are staff shortages and minor delays may occur.

Personnel will be trained for the different restaurant system areas. This allows for cover and effective running of the business model.

Allen Mbengeranwa

The Market & Marketing

3.0 Market research

A questionnaire was used as part of the market research to:
1. Establish potential customers
2. Identify purchase frequency
3. Evaluate the effect of alcohol on restaurant food sales
4. Establish the viability of the business model and concept
5. Gather information for the lifetime value of customers

The method of selecting respondents was random. This involved interviewing every third or immediately after person who appeared over 18 years of age. This age was chosen as some of the questions where alcohol related.

No.	Question	Yes	No	Total
1	Do you eat out more than once a week?	30		30
2	Do you eat grilled beef burgers when out?	28	2	30
3	Do you eat grilled chicken when out?	28	2	30
4	Do you spend more than £5 for a meal out?	30		30
5	Must you have alcohol when eating out?	1	29	30
6	Do you prefer grilled to deep fried chicken?	30		30
7	Do you prefer variety to restaurant meals?	30		30
8	Do you prefer free refills?	30		30
9	Would you take wine to a restaurant for £2?	29	1	30
10	Can you eat a vegemince burger?	25	5	30
11	Grilled fish steaks?	28	2	30
12	Do you eat out with someone?	30		30
13	Do you eat out in groups of 3 plus?	30		30
14	Do you buy takeaways?	30		30
15	Do you repeat good restaurants?	30		30
16	Do you recommend restaurants to others?	30		30
17	Do you like ambient music in restaurants?	30		30
18	Do you buy a drink with your meal?	30		30
	TOTAL	499	41	540

Total respondents: 30   Questionnaire conducted in December 2005

Figure 3 Market Research

Allen Mbengeranwa

The results show that there is a demand for this concept of restaurant. They also show that the restaurant may be able to generate repeat business.

The availability of free refills appears to be very attractive and a motivator that will carve a niche in the market and create barriers for both incumbents and potential market entrants.

Offering the corkage will also be a barrier to entry for potential competitors and incumbents. This facility reduces the cost of meals for customers and appeared to be very popular indeed.

Other research methods

There was a large amount of desk research conducted. This involved reading local newspapers, national papers, industry publications and material available on-line.

The research also included observing local, independent operators and national chains. This activity included gauging customer numbers, analysing the menus and operational features. This activity also centred on establishing the type of customers that the competitors have and the nature of dining that was undertaken.

The information obtained has been collated and evaluated to establish as accurate a picture as possible of the market.

3.1. The Market

Measurability

The intended customers are in the Bangor and surrounding area. The population of Bangor is estimated at 13,725 in 2001. Furthermore, the student population is estimated at 7,500.

Bangor boosts one of the longest High Streets in Britain which attracts many locals from the surrounding areas. The high street is exceptionally busy during the afternoon and there's a vibrant night life.

The following table also summarises the population demographics:

Community Areas	Population	0-15	16 - 19	20 - 29	30 - 59	60 - 74	75 & Over
Bangor	13725	2257	1425	3617	4084	1424	918

Figure 4 Market Demographics

Generation Y – this group includes people born between 1980 and 2000. This is the most ethnically diverse group of people and is estimated to be between two and three times larger than any other group. This group will be targeted as they are also said to be more likely to eat fast food services.

We will reach this market by offering grilled meat as opposed to fried. To cater for their ethical awareness, we will be offering a

Allen Mbengeranwa

range of sauces and Papa's spicy rice. The hamburger is the traditional favourite of this group.

Generation X – this group cover those born between 1965 and 1977. These are classed as young adults and with a need for strong family ties and more likely to focus on their relationships with their children. It is also said that this generation prefers casual convenient establishments to more formal upscale restaurants. They also concerned with value and favour quick service restaurants and mid-scale operations. This market is served by a comfortable atmosphere that focuses on value and ambience.

We will reach the generation X market by offering descent children's meals and value for money. Our menu is made entirely of grilled food stuffs with the fries being reduced in fat and drained before serving.

Accessibility

We will be able to communicate with these customers in a number of ways. We will be able to produce leaflets to deliver to the households, as a form of communication to educate potential customers of our location and services.

We will also produce advertisements in the local paper, The Guardian, which is delivered to the individual houses in Bangor and Anglesey.

We will also access the local market by offering 10% of to the emergency services.

We will access the public sector employees by offering a free meal for two to a nominated individual.   This individual will be nominated by the human resources departments with one from the Local Authority and another from the NHS.

Size

The market research puts the potential market, per household, at 20,000.00. We are assuming that there will be one family per household. The number of economically active persons is 45,804, Gwynedd. This represents a large proportion of people likely to purchase our services, and that of competitors. It is not possible to establish the exact number of people who eat out and how often they do. Bangor is also host to a number of local schools and colleges that also create a market for dinner time meals and after school snacks.
The average spend has been assumed to be £10 per head, on a night out.

Open to practical development

The restaurant will be able to cater for people from 5 and above. The figures show that the market is open to practical development as evident by the other restaurants already established in the industry.   There are no evident barriers to entry from the customers or incumbents.

Allen Mbengeranwa

The market research activities have highlighted the following groups:
1. 5 – 17 years (teens)
2. 18 – 25 years (teens and young couples)
3. 26 – 49 (including those with young families)
4. 50 + (including those with alder families)

This does not mean that the omitted age groups do not eat out, they were not highlighted in our market research.
The market can also be classified as follows:
1. Regular diners (at least once a week)
2. "If nothing else will do…" (socialites)
3. Reluctant diners
4. Non- diners

Psycho-Demographics
Our market philosophy will be to meet the social aspirations and 'belongingness' by eating out with friends. The customers may also want to dine with us as a treat because they feel they deserve it. The Papa Bengie's ™restaurant will enable the target market to achieve their self-esteem and status needs.

This will be possible as established research and evidence available has shown that the individuals will strive to join a social group that is more reflective of their perceived or aspirational social status.

Customer benefits and Problems solved

The restaurant market in Bangor is limited and there is no Italian restaurant in the locality. The market is characterised by having a few restaurants that serve the community. The nearest Italian restaurant is by the peer which means it does not compete with the high street foot fall. There are a number of pubs that offer pub meals and drinks.

The absence of a multiplex cinema and other night leisure activities leads to the main focus of the night life being bars and restaurants. Bangor boasts the biggest capacity to entertain in the local area leading to a majority of the community attending the local night scene from various areas.
This illustrates the need in Bangor for an entertainment experience that is pleasurable and brings the community together in a comfortable and pleasant environment.

We will meet and facilitate for the residents to gather in their social groups and express their need for affection, receiving and giving. This is true of the need for everyone to be appreciated and involved.

The choice of a restaurant eating out experience is affected by four main factors, from the research:
1. Group composition
2. Mental and physical energy
3. location
4. Deals and events

Allen Mbengeranwa

Group composition

The market research has highlighted that the captive audience is more likely to engage in an eating out experience with friends and family. The Italian restaurant business concept is more associated with a romantic meal of reasonable quality. This means that the group spend will be much higher and the size of the restaurant will facilitate for the more intimate of meals and a cosy atmosphere between friends.

Mental and physical energy

Some respondents are highly motivated to experience eating out and encourage friends to join them. However, the research also highlighted that some may be tired after work and reserve going out till the end of the week. However, the type of restaurant will not be too taxing on the customers and we will not be playing loud music that one would not like to hear at the end of a busy day.

Location

As with restaurants, location is vital. The restaurant is located in the north –end of the high street which is dominated by pubs and restaurants. This area is the most vibrant at night. The restaurant is also close to the junction with Bangor Cathedral making it highly visible from the high street consumers.

The high street is served by an underground city centre car park as well as a local car park to the 'entertainment' end of the high street.

The area is also serviced by a range of hair dressers and barber shops, in addition to the other local stores including off-licences, accountants and estate agents, solicitors and department stores. This will provide a good opportunity to market the restaurant and provide exposure.

Deals and events

The restaurant concept offers a 'bottomless' soft drink that customers can access as much as they want. This will be achieved by charging £1.90 for the soft drink and the customers can refill as much as they like. The average consumption is estimated at two glasses per adult customer.

The supplementary services will also enhance the appeal of the core product. This will provide the options of either purchasing the core product on its own, or with the supplements.

We will also offer 10% off for local emergency in uniform from the Police, NHS and Fire brigade. This is designed to generate sales through increase local rapport and generating word of mouth advertising.

The restaurant concept targeting the casual dining market allows us to open for lunch and not offer a separate menu. Customers will still be able to have 'bottomless' soft drinks during all open hours.

Allen Mbengeranwa

The service in customers terms – Papa Bengie's.

➢ *Features*

A menu featuring grilled hamburgers and grilled chicken with various sauces and accompaniments.

Benefits

Our customers will have a large choice of meals and are able to satisfy their individual tastes and circumstances.

Proofs

By only serving grilled dishes from a set menu, we will ensure that the customers are able to choose what they want and anticipate their meal.

➢ *Features*

Table service with counter payments.

Benefits

This allows customers to come and dine when they want, without having to make reservations. Paying at the counter allows the customers to be served quickly and help themselves to sauces and 'bottomless drinks while they wait. This system also allows the customer to know exactly how much their meal will cost.

Proof

There will be table numbers and signs showing customers how to order. The drinks machine will be in view of everyone to help themselves once they have paid and received their glasses. The food will be delivered to their tables, all at once.

> *Features*

A fixed menu displaying all the dishes in the window. We will also have a website showing the menu and services available.

Benefits

This will allow the customers to be able to choose their meals before coming to the restaurant. It will also make it easier for customers to make their decisions when it comes to choosing their meal.

Proof

The menu will be displayed in the window of the restaurant and will be available to take away. A website will also be created to allow customers to view the menu and also act as a contact point. This will later be tied in with the online reservation system.

> *Features*

A quick-service restaurant model with free refills.

Benefits

The quick service of food will allow for customers to get their meals hot and within a reasonable time. The customers will be able to get their main meals moments after the starter. The customers will be able to order their food, eat and engage in other activities that they may have planned for the night.

Free refills will also tempt customers to our restaurant as this is perceived as value for money. The customers can drink as much as they like.

Allen Mbengeranwa

Proofs

As the food will be part prepared, or fully prepared, the service will be quick as the food preparation time is reduced. The dishes will be marinated beforehand to allow maximum flavour and customer experience through taste.

A free refills post-mix station is available for customers to help themselves.

➢ *Features*

'Bring your own wine.

Benefits

This allows the customers to bring their own chosen bottle of wine to accompany their meal. This makes it cheaper for them as they will only pay a £2.50 corkage fee.

The customers will also be able to view our menu and other wines so that they are informed of our service should they want to return for a night out.

Proofs

The offer will be advertised on the menu and included in the communications of the restaurant.

Innovators (First customers)

Our principle customers will be those we have classed as the regular dinners. These diners already exist as evident by the market incumbents. We will aim to attract these diners by advertising and marketing through hair Salons among other avenues. The business concept means that these diners are likely to be 20 years and above living in the local area and with a regular income.

The following describes the factors that are important in the customer's decision to buy or not to buy our service, how much they should buy and how frequently:

Product considerations

➢ Price-

We will be reflective of the clientele we are attracting. The business model and the menu plus services offered will allow us to offer competitive prices. We will also be purchasing the food stuffs part made and ready-made allowing us to benefit from the economies of scale that are associated with large manufacturers.

➢ Quality –

As our food will be outsourced from reputable suppliers who use economies of scale and scope to produce food of constantly high quality and taste. The salad items will be fresh and this will be presented to the customers as they are added on the burgers. The marinades are also prepared to the same consistency so that customers get the same high standard of service.

➢ Appearance-

The premises will be kept clean and tidy with the décor reflecting the type of food and service that is associated with the business model.

Allen Mbengeranwa

The Competition

Direct competitors	Type of food	Family friendly	Student friendly	Average cost of meal
Brewers Fayre Parc Brittannia, Parc Menai	Various	√	√	£6
China Garden Ty Golchi, Caernarfon Rd	Chinese	√	√	£7
Eastern Origin 9, High St	Chinese	√	√	Three course Lunch - £5 Evening - £7
Fat Cat Cafe Bar 161, High St	Various	no children	√	£8
Garden Hotel 1, High St	Chinese	√	√	£6.80
Greek Taverna Politis 12-14, Holyhead Rd	Greek	no children	√	£7.50
Herbs 162, High St	Various (Mediterranean, European, Thai, Pasta, Curry)	√	√	£10
Java Restaurant Ltd 236, High St	A range of International cuisine	√	√	£8
La Bella Vita 166, High St	Italian	√	√	£6-£8
Mahabharat Balti Restaurant 5-7, High St	Indian	√	√	£5.95
Oswalds Restaurant Bryn Haul, Victoria Drive	Various	√	√	Lunch from £7.75 Evening under £17
Papillon 347a, High St	Various	√	√	£6
Ristorante Pulcinella Pier Promenade, Garth Road	Italian	√	√	£6-£8
Royal Tandoori 111, High St	Indian	√	√	£8

Figure 5 Direct Competition Research

46 Restaurant Business Plan – The Complete Format

Pricing

Our pricing ranges from £1.50 for individual items to £6.10 for a combination amounting to a main meal. We will also offer a boned quarter chicken with two chosen side dishes for £4.90. This amounts to a customer saving of £1.00 from the separate purchase price.

We will be relatively cheaper because we offer one price for the complete meal as opposed to the Chinese and Indian restaurants that have a separate price for the main dish sauce and an additional charge for the rice and/or noodles. This means that the restaurants ultimately have a higher total price but their meals will be more expensive compared to our one price for a dish pricing policy.

Customers will be able to choose additional accompaniments to their meal and a 'bottomless drink' at £1.90 will be highly attractive.

Competitor's reactions

We have built in a fall-back position as the market is unable to cut prices. There are many 'Chicken fast food restaurants' such as KFC that offer customer's cheap chicken for £2 to £5. The high fat content and single flavour will act as a disadvantage to them. We offer healthier grilled foods with a customer's choice of sauce.

Allen Mbengeranwa

Our meals will also be prepared fresh and to order resulting in a higher quality meal and customer experience.

By lowering their prices, the chicken and burger outlets will then fall into what is perceived to be an inferior market bracket associated with low quality, unhygienic ingredients and premises.

All our meals will be of constant quality and customers can expect the same level of experience and taste time and again.
This makes us cheaper than Pizza Hut in range and our customers will be able to dine with us for a cheaper and yet more superior meals and dining experience.

Our Hamburgers are handmade and may come with two sides, to constitute a full main course. Our chicken is also boned which allows customers to enjoy the product and take advantage of the added flavour of marinating with no bones.

This makes our pricing policy relatively cheap compared to other restaurant main meals. We also have a selection of quality enhancing presentations such as adding side sauces after grilling the chicken or hamburger for more added value. Market research has shown that using fresh ingredients for presentations also enhances the value and the amount customers are willing to pay for fresh products.

3.2. SWOT Analysis

Competitors' Strengths and Weaknesses.

The competitors are already established within the local market. This gives them an advantage as the incumbents. The geographical market is well served as the competitors are spread throughout the County in and around the town centre.

The direct competitors include JD Weatherspoon's, a pub and also KFC. They are strong in the offers available to customers including a choice of battered chicken and provide pints with their meals.

The major disadvantage is that KFC is mostly a take-away venue with six plastic tables where the customers can sit while they wait for their food. This does not classify the outlet as a restaurant.

It will be easy to take market share from this incumbent as we will offer clients an opportunity to have their meals within the restaurant or to take away. This is a highly effective strategy that is already used by other restaurateurs.

Our competitive edge is the menu, the environment and service delivery model. We have a marketing campaign that our competitors will not offer. We will also be able to produce our food fast and fresh to meet the customer demands quickly, effectively and customer friendly.

Allen Mbengeranwa

Opportunities

The competition is focused on serving different market segments to those that we intend to target. Pizza Hut is targeted at family diners, in Llandudno Junction as outlined by their menu design and the offers that they have. The KFC outlet take away restaurant targets the takeaway market and offers no dining facilities.

We aim to serve the evening diners as our core target market. This is illustrated by our emphasis on service, environment and consistent high quality food. Our location, which is close to the parking spaces close to the high street and allows us to offer a dinning service as our customers are able to drive and park their vehicle while they dine with us.

There is currently no restaurant in the local area that offers free refills for drinks. The market research has proved this to be very popular and likely to increase the chances of customers dining with us. This will create a barrier to entry into the market for other restaurateurs. This will also take significant market share from the incumbents.

Threats

The premises are still available on the open market. There is a risk that they may be taken off the market and occupied by someone else. We will not be able to start-up at the preferred location.

Competitor's reactions

We have built in a fall-back position although the market is unable to cut prices. The 'Chicken fast food restaurants' such as KFC, that offer customer's reportedly cheap chicken from £1.99 to £10.00. These are relatively cheap chicken meals where the customers have to choose between two and four accompaniments. The chicken used is said to be also of inferior quality and the resulting product is also of inferior quality.

By lowering their prices, the pubs houses will then fall into this allegedly inferior market bracket associated with low quality, unhygienic ingredients and premises.

3.3. Competitive Advantage

We will be offering an evening experience not currently available within the local market. The geographical layout of the area warrants for a deviation from focusing on foot flow alone. We will be marketing our Unique selling Propositions and engaging in cross selling through local small businesses.

Our service creation model has allowed us to focus on the customers. We will aim to serve our clients and treat them with the greatest of customer care rather than relying on our food to sell for us. This brings about the billion dollar question, 'how many people can make a better beef burger than McDonalds?'

We have the intention of creating a brand by distinguishing our restaurant through marketing, sales activities and focus on customer care. We will listen to our customers by constantly asking them if they like their meal and if they have any comments.

Allen Mbengeranwa

The plan is to have the restaurant as aesthetically pleasing as possible while focussing on the desired image and restaurant concept. We will be an evening dining restaurant with afternoon sales, excellent systems and customer care.

The location is also excellent for driving customers as there are public car parks nearby.

3.4. Marketing Strategy

Current market

The local market is characterised by Pubs, chicken, Chinese and Indian fast food restaurants. There are places that serve Hamburgers and inferior chicken but there is no provision for dining. The products on offer are also aimed at the fast food market. There is no restaurant currently serving quality fresh, convenient hamburgers and grilled chicken within a dining environment.

Benefits of our service

We will serve fresh grilled Hamburgers plus chicken and a range of side dishes to the market. Our environment will be stimulating and presenting an aesthetic environment for quality dining.

Customer needs we will fill

There are no quality dining restaurants serving grilled hamburgers and chicken dishes in the Gwynedd area. The market is littered with Pubs, fast food, 'chicken and kebab' restaurants.

We will offer an alternative and become one of the few quality restaurants in the area. This niche will allow us to generate enough customers to continue to offer our customers value for money.

Allen Mbengeranwa

Marketing and Advertising objectives

We aim to raise awareness of our market presence and products and services offered. We aim to be included when our target market is considering making their buying decisions to eat in a restaurant or treat themselves or a loved one. We aim to be included when our target market is considering treating themselves or spending time satisfying their sociological and emotional needs through eating out.

Additional costs of achieving marketing and advertising objectives

A fixed cost figure of £300 per month will aimed for. We will aim for 'below the line' advertising. This is consistent with new businesses and is known to be more effective for our target market.

Method
The restaurant should be available as a choice at the start of the consumer purchase decision path. When our target market is evaluating eating out, they will consider the type of environment and service they wish to experience. We wish to be present at this stage.

We will offer student discounts and discounts to emergency services on duty.

This method will cost us £1 in every £10 and is consistent with the traditional method of spending 10% of the previous year's sales.

This method results in high spending after a good year and so on. As a start-up, our method is the best as it allows us to offer the advertising spend along with sales. The overall effect is that for 10% of marketing we get 90%, upfront. It will also be extremely effective to monitor the effectiveness of this method.

It is also an easy system to administer and is a highly effective above the line marketing and advertising method.

The decision is also made in other areas and times. An example is at the end of the working day after a good or bad days work. Having a captive audience at this stage is difficult. We will however, have a sustained marketing plan that will allow for our target market to be constantly informed of our services. This sustained activity will allow for our customers to evaluate us given the experiences they seek having encountered us through above the line advertising and marketing.

The message we will convey through literature and other promotions is that we will offer a dining environment of quality food and service. When our target market wishes to treat themselves to quality ingredients, excellent service and pleasant experiences they will be aware of us. We will highlight our grilled Hamburgers and boned chicken individually made to order with the freshest ingredients. We will also have friendly employees that undergo regular training and appraisals to maintain customer service standards to the desired high level.

Our complaints handling will also be used as a marketing and advertising initiative. We will offer replacement meals that will resolve the customer's complaints to show that we have listened and are able to respond to requests.

The focus will be on trying to create a strong peer-to-peer marketing campaign by creating a service that generates excellent experiences for our customers. By meeting, and continually exceeding their expectations with regard to emotions and feelings we will be associated with pleasant experiences that will generate conversations. This advertising is crucial and priceless.

The décor will also be of high quality as the restaurant will be new and many of the materials will be aesthetically pleasing and delightful to the eye. There will be simple décor with quality tables and chairs, minimal artwork and ambient lighting. The lighting is also known as mood lighting.

In conclusion, customers should by from us because we – the restaurant- are different. We will offer a niche service focused on customer care with emphasis on goodwill and pleasant behaviour, especially mannerisms.

Customers should buy from us because it – the food – is different. We will have a selection of main meals that will be consistently high in quality. We will also be offering fresh grilled Hamburgers and chicken made to order with the freshest ingredients. We have a combination of presentation styles and techniques that will differentiate the grilled chicken. We will use fresh sauces and presentations. We will not smother all our quality food in cheap genetically modified ingredients and leave customers guessing what is in their food.

Media

Yellow pages
We will use the yellow pages to place a free advert that is offered to all businesses.

There will also be an editorial that will be sent to the local guardian free paper.
There is a price list included. This is also the menu and will be available to take away by customers.

There is a plan to create a discount list that features 'the blue lights'. This will be a service that will be offered to members of the emergency services. The Fire brigade, police and ambulance staff will get a 10% discount with their meals. This will be done by sending a letter to the offices/bases of the services informing them of the discount.

There is also a plan to sponsor a media competition by offering the winner a free meal if they win. This will allow for us to get some above the line advertising. A description of what is available will be offered to entice entrance to the competition offering a free quality meal.

In order to get our target market, we will have to leaflet the local area through either inserts or loose leaflets. This is best done at the local train station and may be cheap and highly effective for rush hours

Allen Mbengeranwa

Marketing and Advertising competitive difference

We will be the only restaurant to offer Local Area Businesses Marketing through Hair Salons and barbers. This is unlike our competitors.

We will also offer a blue lights discount which is the first of its kind in the local restaurant area.

We will also engage in competitions and giveaways which are not currently practised by the incumbents.

Service creation

There are a number of factors that come together to create the service and deliver it to the customers. The relationship between these factors and how they combine is best illustrated by means of a diagram:

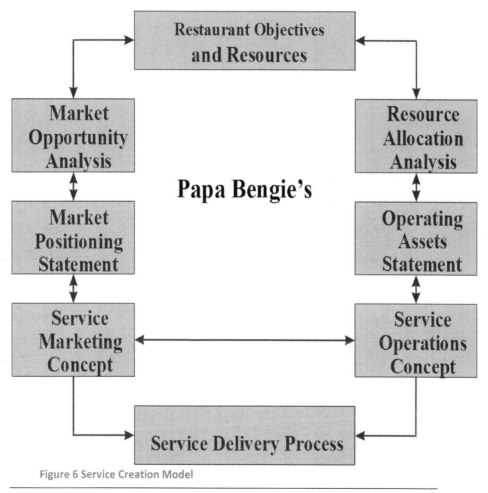

Figure 6 Service Creation Model

Allen Mbengeranwa

Before the detailed description of the service creation and delivery model for the restaurant, the outline is that the food to be served to customers will be purchased from suppliers and prepared, presented and served in the restaurant. The material is available in full in other parts of this plan.

There will also be service designed to enhance and facilitate the service delivery. It will be necessary to run payroll and administrative functions to facilitate the service. These will also include encounters with various council departments and other public bodies such as the Revenue and Customs.

The Sales plan

The service will be sold within the restaurant. We will not be engaging salesman or making sales calls. We will be relying on our marketing activities to drive sales and generate revenue.

The ingredients will be purchased in relation to stock levels and anticipated sales. This will allow us to offer a fast service and monitors sales easily and effectively. The meals will be presented on white plates and cutlery available.

The selling of the service will also be down to the presentation and service style of the staff. All staff will be trained on the menu and the beverages available. They will also be tested and trained on customer service.

The marketing activities that are designed to drive local sales by attracting and generating repeat custom from the local residents.

Our pricing is based on the costs associated with purchasing the products from suppliers. We aim to have a pricing policy that will maintain a low price for our meals while generating sufficient sales to keep operating. The menu consists of combination meals which are cheaper than when the items are purchased individually.

Sales plan: Grand opening

The shop front will be fabricated before the opening. This is designed to increase and maintain the visibility of the store. This is of low cost and has been proven to be a highly successful strategy.

The will also be an opening night event where we will invite local business, council officials, local press and local groups. As we are a start-up, we will ask all those that wish to attend to make a contribution of £5 to cover a buffet starter, main course and refreshments.

Sales Plan: Point of Purchase (P.O.P)

We will use leaflets placed by the door and on table tops to explain the services available, including the way food should be ordered. We will also have takeaway menus for customers to take away. The quick service restaurant model chosen reduces the need for large numbers of service staff and reduced waste through mix-ups and delays. This is similar to restaurants like Nandos, McDonalds, J D Weatherspoon's, Burger King and most pubs that

Allen Mbengeranwa

may have a brand in their sauces which they are able to sell to customers.

Sales Plan: Direct mail piece and press campaign

We will use a leaflet that will highlight the opening of the restaurant and the menu that is on offer. This will be included in the local papers as a leaflet so as to target the local residents. The aim of this campaign will be to make it in conjunction with a press release in order to gain the maximum exposure and possible sales. The press release will highlight the Handmade nature of the Hamburgers, the Grilled chicken and the wide ranging menu on offer at a quick and friendly restaurant.

Sales Plan: Local store marketing

We aim to offer a discount to the local students and emergency services in uniform. This is designed to create a relationship with the residents and increase the sales avenues for our restaurant. We will also aim to present a 'free' meal for one nominated Pensioner every month. This will be designed and marketed as an OAP scheme that will generate interest and exposure within the local services. To be eligible, the OAP's will have to register on a list with us.

Sales Plan: 'Bring your own wine'

We will charge £2.00 for customers to bring their own chosen wines. This allows the customers to 'save' on the wine while enjoying a quality meal.

This allows us to offer value for money. This Sales plan will work because there is an Outlet Selling wines and other alcoholic drinks. It is located just yards away allowing our customers to just nip in before they dine with us. They can also purchase wines from their supermarkets.

Future markets

There is a strong possibility for a delivery service. This will allow us to serve within the restaurant and also deliver to customers. There will be an opportunity to spread the fixed assets over other services such as a lunch opening and catering service to the local area and Gwynedd.

Industry and market watch

There will be a subscription to the Restaurant magazine and the Caterer and Hotelier magazine. This will allow us to be in touch with the restaurant market. We will also participate in the Regional business support programmes and join the local small business forum.

Place and distribution

The chosen location has a ground floor area of 789 sq. ft. There are also offices above the sales area of 144sq.ft. These may be used as staff facilities and offices. The location also has a kitchen with access to a basement.

Allen Mbengeranwa

The restaurant may be located in quieter areas of the high street as this fits in with the target market who will not want to associate with the binge drinking culture of high street pubs and clubs.

The chosen location, 208 High Street, Bangor occupies a prime retail location within the pedestrianised section of the high street, close to many multiples including W H Smiths, Littlewoods and Debenhams. Bangor is the principle shopping centre for the county of Gwynedd and Anglesey and thus enjoys a wide catchment area in addition to being a University City.

Location type advantages

This location offers a competitive advantage in that the area suits the target market. It is calm with a high foot flow and is very close to car parking areas. It is also close to other pubs and restaurants as well as high street shops. This allows for the restaurant to be complemented by these other services. There is also a double screen cinema in the town.

The premises create the desired atmosphere and the size allows us to charge less for our quality food making us more competitive.

Premises

The chosen location is 208 High Street, Bangor. The premises will need an A3 licence estimated at £300.00. It is necessary to apply for this permission as the premises are currently listed as shop/show room.

Size of premises:

Ground floor sales area:	789 sq. ft.
Office accommodation:	144 sq. ft.
Separate WC	
Kitchen with access to basement	

The office accommodation is spread over first second and third floors with independent access.

The location has been selected based on the following criteria:
1. Community size
2. High visibility
3. Available parking spaces
4. Good public transport links
5. Mid to low cost premises
6. Mixed income community make-up
7. No overabundance of direct competition in the trade area.

Allen Mbengeranwa

State of repair of premises:

The premises are reported as requiring some refurbishment. The premises will need to be converted into restaurant accommodation on the ground floor.

1. shop front and sliding doors   £1,200.00
2. tills and service area refurbishment   £1,000.00
3. air conditioning units   £2,000.00
4. Sound system   £500.00
5. Dining area refurbishment   £3,000.00
6. CCTV system   £500.00
7. Greeting station   £50.00
8. Electric kitchen extractor   £2,000.00
9. kitchen fly killers   £148.06
10. Post mix systems   £free
11. Kitchen storage shelves (Dry)   £100.00

Cost of improvements and repair: £10,498.06

Tenure: Freehold

The rateable value of the premises is £11,282.80 with the county of Gwynedd and includes the offices rated separately at £2,652.30.

The premises are available for sale at £375.000.00

Figure 7 Premises

Capital Expenditure

1.1. Equipment required

1.	Kitchen Prep Stations and tables		£300.00
2.	Contact grills	x4	£2,024.64
3.	Commercial fryers	x2	£1,018.00
4.	Commercial fridge	x1	£574.58
5.	Commercial freezer	x1	£821.33
6.	Dish washers	x1	£1,055.00
7.	Microwave ovens	x2	£1,174.98
8.	Commercial rice cooker	x1	£142.56
9.	Tables (chairs)	x25(50)	£2,000.00
10.	baby seats	x3	£50.00
11.	Plates	x50	£319.50
12.	Forks and Knives	x50 sets	£120.00
13.	Drinking Glasses	x100	£200.00
14.	Wine glasses	x20	£50.00
15.	Salad plates	x20	£100.00
16.	Serving trays	x5	£25.00
17.	Sauce drizzle bottles	x7	£7.00
18.	Food hygiene prep board	x6	£15.00
19.	Salt and Pepper shakers	x60	£40.00
20.	Cleaning materials	various	£100.00
21.	Tills and software	x2	£2,000.00
22.	hand held floor aid	x2	£300.00
23.	Computer and printer	x1	£695.00
24.	accounting software	x1	£695.00
25.	Office consumables	various	£100.00
26.	Commercial vehicle	L200	£18,763.30
	TOTAL Equipment costs		£32,690.89

Figure 8 Equipment Required

Allen Mbengeranwa

1.1. Start Up Costs

1. Solicitors fees   £2,000.00
2. A3 planning permission   £300.00
3. Marketing   £700.00
4. *Opening stock*   *£1,000,00*
5. *Insurance*   *£1,000.00*
6. *Wages – 1 month*   *£4,000.00*
7. *Rates – I month*   *£940.00*
8. Manuals   x3   £600.00

TOTAL START UP COSTS   £10,540.00

Figure 9 Start Up Costs

1.0 Staffing Requirements

1. Assistant manger (experienced)   Full time hours
2. Grill station one   full time hours
3. Tills one   Full time hours
4. Till relief/customer service relief   Part –time hours
5. Food Prep station one   Part-time hours
6. Floor customer service one   Part-time hours
7. Floor customer service two   Part-time hours

Remuneration rates:
1.0 Assistant manager   £16,900.00
Staff rate one   £6/hr

Figure 10 Staffing Requirements

Employees will have to have at least 6 months experience in a restaurant or food service environment.

The assistant manager will be required to have or be willing to undergo Food Safety and Hygiene training. The preferred candidate will have hospitality and catering qualifications.

All staff will be assessed at interview and any training required identified. Staff handbooks will also be issued and there is a probation period of 6 months.

The minimum staffing level is 3. More staff will be recruited as the business grows and the full time hours may be made of up part time employees with a few hours each.

Allen Mbengeranwa

Legal Aspects

3.5. Business Status

Papa Bengie's ™is a brand name for The Owners Management Limited. The business and outlet will be owned and operated by The Owners Management limited.

3.6. Other Legal Requirements

A3 Planning permission at £300.00

4.0 Insurance

A complete insurance package including:

Employer's liability,

Public liability,

Buildings and Contents insurance at £1,000.00 per annum.

Financial Information

4.1. Pricing Method

Prices have been arrived at by comparing with those of the competition and having at least 100% mark-up on cost price. Some menu items have greater margins. The menu is focused on meal combinations that have higher total revenue for us, offering customers a lower group price. This is similar to the restaurant standards.

4.2. Payment Method

➢ Suppliers – There are no credit terms assumed to be available from suppliers.
➢ Customers – There are no payment terms offered to customers except cash when ordering. Chip and pin will be available for customers.

4.3. Survival budget/Personal Drawings

Total monthly expenses
£1,000.00

Allen Mbengeranwa

4.4. Break even Calculation

1.1. Break even Calculation

Turnover	£159,000.00
Less	
Direct costs	£9,000.00
Gross Profit	£150,000.00

Gross Profit margin (%)	(£150,000.00/£159,000.00)*100=94.33%

Gross Profit	£150,000.00
Less	
Fixed costs year 1	£214,812.36
Net Profit (Loss)	(£64,812.36)

Break even sales	£214,812.36*(100/94.33) = 227,724.33

Break even sales	227,724.33

Monthly break even sales	18,977.03

The Break even sales do not take into account the interest payments rebate on the payments made.

The fixed costs are very high as there is a charge of £90,000.00 per annum in order to pay off the £450,000.00 in five years. This is assumed to be all debt and the effective interest rate amounts to £25,000.00 per year flat rate.

Figure 11 Break even calculation

Sales Forecast

1.1. Sales Forecast

	Price	Month 1	Months 2-8&11	Months 7-10&12
Meal	£4.90	0	£9,800.00	£11,760.00
Drink	£1.90	0	£3,800.00	£4,560.00
Total		0	£13,600.00	£16,320.00

Total annual sales: - £159,000.00.

Figure 12 Sales Forcast

Allen Mbengeranwa

4.5. Cash flow forecast

See appendix for year one and two, a summary is included below:

A Pro Forma two year cash flow statement is included below:

Cash Flow Sheet	2006/7 Total	2007/8 Total
Projected Sales	159,000.00	190,300.00
Cash Receipts (Cash In)		
Sales Invoiced	159,000.00	190,300.00
Catering	0	8,600
Interest rebate	23,523.00	20,700.00
Loan Proceeds	450,000.00	0
Other cash received	0	0
	0	0
Total Cash In	632,523.00	219,600.00
Cash Disbursments (Cash out)	0	0
Purchases (direct expenses)	9,000.00	12,000.00
Advertising	3,600.00	3,600.00
Cars incl. Insurance)	1,200.00	1,200.00
Bank Charges	0	0
Loan Interest	51,750.00	41,400.00
Insurance (Business Liability)	1,000.00	1,000.00
Professional Fees (Accounting & Legal)	2,000.00	500.00
Rent (Equipment)	0	0
Rent (Premises) + Rates	11,283.00	11,283.00
Telephone and fax	160.00	160.00
Utilitites	6,000.00	6,000.00
Repairs & Maintenance	0	0
Marketing	3,600.00	3,600.00
Travel & Promotion	0	0
Wages (Employees & payroll deductions)	38,403.00	41,894.00
Management Salaries	0	0
Loan Payments (capital NOT interest)	79,000.00	90,000.00
Purchase Fixed Assets	419,789.00	0
Taxes (Income)	0	0
Office Supplies & Expenses	600.00	600.00
	0	0
Total Cash Out	627,384.00	213,237.00
Cash Flow Summary		
Opening Balance	0	5,138.00
Add: Cash In	632,523.00	219,600.00
Subtract: Cash Out	627,384.00	213,237.00
Surplus or (Deficit)	5,138.00	6,363.00
Closing Cash Balance	5,138.00	11,501.0

Figure 13 Cash Flow Forecast

4.6. Cash flow forecast assumptions

The restaurant assumes 500 meals a week, in the slow months. This includes lunch meals, take away and evening meals over a 7 day period. 80% of the sales will be on Friday Night, Saturday day and Night and Sunday.

The second period of sales volumes is assumed to fall during school breaks and the beginning of the university academic year.

The average revenue per meal is £7.

The average cost of a meal is £1.50.

£90,000.00 annual capital repayment is assumed over five years.

Interest rate is assumed at 11.5% and is calculated over the year.

There is an estimated rebate of 50% the following month after payment.
An increase in sales of 10% is assumed in year two. This will be driven by the constant marketing and advertising activity.

Cash flow risk

There is a significant risk of a cash flow crisis. This is because there are periods of deficits within the first 18 months of

Allen Mbengeranwa

operating. A cash surplus from the estimated start up costs will be used to prevent liquidity problems. This is largely due to the target of paying of £79,000.00 of the borrowed funds in the first year.

Interest burden

The high gearing also means that the interest payments will be very high in the first year, reducing as the balance outstanding is reduced. There is a target to pay off all the borrowings within the 5th year. The interest risk is necessary to ensure the long-term survival of the business and not short term profitability with perpetual haemorrhaging of cash.

Financial Disciplines

The use of the market leading accounting software will ensue that the financial position is monitored on a real time basis with daily frequency for the first three months of operating.

The use of comprehensive restaurant software also allows for the constant monitoring of the restaurant activities and all factors important to our survival.

There are also manual controls imbedded in the operations manuals and daily management activity such as cash handling, stock and theft management plus waste control.

Survival capabilities

The use of various control, operational, human resources plus management systems and projections outline in the business plan will ensure the survival of the business. The insurance has also been chosen to reduce the risk of interruptions arising from unforeseen events.

Allen Mbengeranwa

Financial Deal

It would be ideal to grow the business through cash flow. This means that the business will have to grow slower than would be ideal. However, this gives the opportunity to refine the business model and make more accurate assumptions and predictions. The ability to return funds to investors is a priority.

As this is a start-up, the cash flow and profit and loss positions will be monitored more closely as the business is cash heavy with no initial credit terms. The chosen software is able to function at his level plus provide even more detailed analysis.

Important assumptions

Important assumptions

The assumptions are based on monthly and annual positions.

%	2005	2006	2007
Tax rate £10-50K	23.75	23.75	23.75
VAT	17.5	17.5	17.5
Interest rates-	11.5%	11.5%	11.5%
National insurance	18	18	18

Figure 14 Financial Assumptions

Exit routes

The business model has potential to be replicated to create a chain of restaurants with the right management team and new finance model. The creation of a strong brand will increase the likelihood of having a trade sale or equity sale in the long run. In the short term, the single unit will increase the value of the property underlining the investment. This will allow the business model to extract value from the property and provide a lump sum return to the investors.

Financing requirements

Financing requirements

The finance required amounts to £450.000.00. The funding is needed to purchase fixed assets, purchase of the lease and other start up expenses. This round of funding does not include any structural works.

Fixed assets
    Cost of improvements and repair: £10,498.06
    The premises   £375.000.00
Capital Expenditure
    Equipment costs   £32,690.89
Start-up costs
    Total   £10,540.00

Total   £428,728.95

Figure 15 Financing Requirements

Allen Mbengeranwa

The other £21,271.05 is needed capital levelling between months 2 and 12. This is because the high interest rates will be draining the cash generated. The balance of the principal amount will reduce every month, however, a constant interest figure is assumed and this is only reduced in the second year. The first year's interest bill is estimated at £51,750.00. There is also an interest rebate estimated at £23,523.00 for the months 3 to 12. This is subject to payments being made on time in the previous month.

The working capital requirements are also very high as the entire funding is assumed to be debt with a repayment period of five years. This amounts to £90,000.00 per year.

Timetable / Milestones

Timetable / Milestones

	Dec	Jan	Feb	Mar	Apr	May	Jun	Jul	Aug	Sep	Oct	Nov
Premises												
Planning	◉											
Fixtures		◉										
Marketing	◉	◉	◉	◉	◉	◉	◉	◉	◉	◉	◉	◉
Launch												
Delivery		◉										
Catering		◉										
Assets		◉										
Lunches												

Milestones	Start Date	End Date	Budget	Responsibility
Premises	16/01/2006	02/03/2006	£375,000.00	Allen
Fixtures	20/02/2006	02/03/2006	£10,498.06	Allen
Marketing	20/02/2006	Ongoing	£300 p/m	Allen
Solicitors fees	02/03/2006		£2,000.00	Allen
Admin & Kit	20/02/2006	Ongoing	£42,230.89	Allen
Launch Stock	18/12/2006	30/03/2006	£1,000.00	Allen
Training	02/003/2006	Ongoing		allen

Figure 16 Timetable/Milestones

Allen Mbengeranwa

Financial information

The financial information has been divided between this section and the appendix. This is because some of the material was not presentable in this section. It has however, been included in the appendix.

The Balance sheet

Papa Bengie's Bangor Balance Sheet	Opening Balance Sheet	Closing Balance Sheet Year 1	Balance Sheet Year 2
Net assets employed			
Fixed Assets			
Premises	£375,000.00	£375,000.00	£375,000.00
Fixtures	£43,188.95	£43,188.95	£38,870.05
Total costs	£418,188.95	£418,188.95	£413,870.05
Accum depreciation	£0	£4,318.90	£3,887.00
Net book value	£418,188.95	**£413,870.05**	£409,983.05
Current assets			
Stock	£1,000.00	£800.00	£800
Bank & Cash	£30,811.05	£5,138.00	£11,501.00
	£31,822.05	£5,938.00	£12,301.00
Current liabilities			
Grants and funding	£0.00	£0.00	£0.00
overdrafts	0	0	0
short-term loan	0	0	0
taxes	0	0	0
Net current assets	£31,822.05	**£5,938.00**	£12,301.00
Total assets less current liabilities	£450,000.00	**£419,808.05**	£422,284.05
Financed by:			
Loan Capital	£450,000.00	£371,000.00	£281,000.00
Called up share Capital		£86,282.15	£138,146.21
Accumulated profits(deficit)		-£37,474.10	£3,137.64

The loan capital is assumed to be coming from various sources:

Loans and equity finance:			**£450,000.00**

Depreciation on fixed assets is assumed at 10% per annum.

Figure 17 Balance Sheet

Allen Mbengeranwa

The Operating Statement

The 12 month operating statement has been included in the appendix. The statement has a number of assumptions associated with it. These are:

- ❖ The restaurant will be operational from the end of March
- ❖ There is an interest rebate estimated at 50% of the previous month's payments.
- ❖ There are no credit arrangements with suppliers or customers
- ❖ The sales have been estimated using the market research evidence. This includes observing the competition in the local area for customer numbers. Although this may not be definitive, it does provide a guide and a yardstick for our sales figures.
- ❖ There is an estimated increase in sales in year two of 10%. This is assumed to be driven by the constant advertising and marketing activities.

A summary Pro Forma Profit and Loss statement covering the upcoming two year period is presented			
Sales		2006/7	2007/8
Restaurant sales		£159,000.00	£190,300.00
Catering		£0.00	£8,600.00
Interest rebate		£23,520.10	£20,700.00
			£0.00
Totals		£182,520.10	£219,600.00
Cost of goods sold		£9,000.00	£12,000.00
Gross Profit		£173,520.10	£207,600.00
Overheads			
Sales Costs		£3,600.00	£3,600.00
Admin Costs		£46,383.00	£46,383.00
Establishment Costs		£100,604.64	£104,422.80
Finance Costs		£60,406.56	£50,056.56
		£0.00	£0.00
Totals		£210,994.20	£204,462.36
Net Profit/Loss		-£37,474.10	£3,137.64
Sales			

Figure 18 Pro Forma Profit and Loss Statement

Allen Mbengeranwa

Appendix

Administration Costs

ADMIN COSTS

Papa Bengie's Bangor - Admin costs	Dec	Jan	Feb	Mar	Apr	May	Jun	Jul	Aug	Sep	Oct	Nov
Salaries	£41,893.68	£3,491.14	£3,491.14	£3,491.14	£3,491.14	£3,491.14	£3,491.14	£3,491.14	£3,491.14	£3,491.14	£3,491.14	£3,491.14
Other Payroll Costs	£4,189.37	£349.11	£349.11	£349.11	£349.11	£349.11	£349.11	£349.11	£349.11	£349.11	£349.11	£349.11
Telephone and fax	£130.00	£0.00	£32.50	£0.00	£0.00	£32.50	£0.00	£0.00	£32.50	£0.00	£0.00	£32.50
Office Consumables	£0.00	£0.00	£0.00	£0.00	£0.00	£0.00	£0.00	£0.00	£0.00	£0.00	£0.00	£0.00
Subscriptions	£50.00	£4.17	£4.17	£4.17	£4.17	£4.17	£4.17	£4.17	£4.17	£4.17	£4.17	£4.17
Investors	£0.00	£0.00	£0.00	£0.00	£0.00	£0.00	£0.00	£0.00	£0.00	£0.00	£0.00	£0.00
Publications	£0.00	£0.00	£0.00	£0.00	£0.00	£0.00	£0.00	£0.00	£0.00	£0.00	£0.00	£0.00
Miscellaneous	£120.00	£10.00	£10.00	£10.00	£10.00	£10.00	£10.00	£10.00	£10.00	£10.00	£10.00	£10.00
TOTALS	£46,383.05	£3,854.42	£3,886.92	£3,854.42	£3,854.42	£3,886.92	£3,854.42	£3,854.42	£3,886.92	£3,854.42	£3,854.42	£3,886.92

Equipment Inventory

Equipment inventory	Size	Make	Quantity	Unit price	VAT	Total Cost
Fridge with digital temperature	770x720x1702		1	£699.00	£122.33	£821.33
Freezer	600x600x1850		1	£489.00	£85.58	£574.58
Plates and bowls			sets			£300.00
Cafetiere			5			£80.00
Electric kettle			1	£20.00		£20.00
Serverware						
Cutlery			sets	£100.00		£100.00
Cutlery tray			1	£2.99	£0.52	£3.51
Table top Menu covers			10	£9.07	N/A	£90.70
Window menu display			1			
Glassware	red , white,water		30	£0.95	£0.17	£33.60
Dishwasher			1	£1,055.00		£1,055.00
Tables and chairs			10			£500.00
Microwave oven			1	£499.99	£87.50	£587.49
Pizza oven			1	£1,100.00		£1,100.00
Fly killers	40 sq.metre		1	£63.00	£11.03	£74.03
Infra red grill	330Hx550wx290D		1	£185.50		£185.50
Stainless steel wall table	900wx700dx900h		1	£175.00		£175.00
Group total						£5,700.74
Structural works						£3,000.00
Food hygiene certificate				£75 per pe		£150.00
Total						£8,850.74
Office admin p.c and furniture						£600.00
Software - sage line 50/One						£695.00
Solicitors fees						£2,000.00
Planning permision						£265.00

Allen Mbengeranwa

Establishment/Property Costs

Costs Summary

Papa Bengie's Bangor - Establishment costs

		Dec	Jan	Feb	Mar	Apr	May	Jun	Jul	Aug	Sep	Oct	Nov
Capital repayments	£86,181.82	£7,181.82	£7,181.82	£7,181.82	£7,181.82	£7,181.82	£7,181.82	£7,181.82	£7,181.82	£7,181.82	£7,181.82	£7,181.82	£7,181.82
Rates	£11,282.80	£940.23	£940.23	£940.23	£940.23	£940.23	£940.23	£940.23	£940.23	£940.23	£940.23	£940.23	£940.23
Insurance	£1,000.00	£83.33	£83.33	£83.33	£83.33	£83.33	£83.33	£83.33	£83.33	£83.33	£83.33	£83.33	£83.33
Telephone	£360.00	£30.00	£30.00	£30.00	£30.00	£30.00	£30.00	£30.00	£30.00	£30.00	£30.00	£30.00	£30.00
Electricity	£1,000.00	£83.33	£83.33	£83.33	£83.33	£83.33	£83.33	£83.33	£83.33	£83.33	£83.33	£83.33	£83.33
Gas	£280.00	£23.33	£23.33	£23.33	£23.33	£23.33	£23.33	£23.33	£23.33	£23.33	£23.33	£23.33	£23.33
Water	£500.00	£41.67	£41.67	£41.67	£41.67	£41.67	£41.67	£41.67	£41.67	£41.67	£41.67	£41.67	£41.67
TOTALS	£100,604.62	£8,383.72	£8,383.72	£8,383.72	£8,383.72	£8,383.72	£8,383.72	£8,383.72	£8,383.72	£8,383.72	£8,383.72	£8,383.72	£8,383.72

NOTES:-

1. Capital Repayment of £86,181.82 per year in lieu of rent
2. Quarterly and Bi-annual costs are illustrated monthly for the first year of trading

88 Restaurant Business Plan – The Complete Format

Finance Costs Year One

Papa Bengie's Bangor - Finance cost year one

Finance Costs

	Dec	Jan	Feb	Mar	Apr	May	Jun	Jul	Aug	Sep	Oct	Nov
Audit and Tax	£0.00	£0.00	£0.00	£0.00	£0.00	£0.00	£0.00	£0.00	£0.00	£0.00	£0.00	£0.00
Other Taxes												
Legal and Professional Fees												
Solicitors	£2,000.00	£166.67	£166.67	£166.67	£166.67	£166.67	£166.67	£166.67	£166.67	£166.67	£166.67	£166.67
Accountants	£1,000.00	£83.33	£83.33	£83.33	£83.33	£83.33	£83.33	£83.33	£83.33	£83.33	£83.33	£83.33
Preference Interest Paid (100)	£0.00	£0.00	£0.00	£0.00	£0.00	£0.00	£0.00	£0.00	£0.00	£0.00	£0.00	£0.00
Bank Interest Paid (50)	£51,750.00	£4,312.50	£4,312.50	£4,312.50	£4,312.50	£4,312.50	£4,312.50	£4,312.50	£4,312.50	£4,312.50	£4,312.50	£4,312.50
Bank Interest Received	£0.00	£0.00	£0.00	£0.00	£0.00	£0.00	£0.00	£0.00	£0.00	£0.00	£0.00	£0.00
VAT	£0.00	£0.00	£0.00	£0.00	£0.00	£0.00	£0.00	£0.00	£0.00	£0.00	£0.00	£0.00
Fixed assets written off	£0.00	£0.00	£0.00	£0.00	£0.00	£0.00	£0.00	£0.00	£0.00	£0.00	£0.00	£0.00
Depreciation	£5,656.59	£471.38	£471.38	£471.38	£471.38	£471.38	£471.38	£471.38	£471.38	£471.38	£471.38	£471.38
Bad Debts	£0.00	£0.00	£0.00	£0.00	£0.00	£0.00	£0.00	£0.00	£0.00	£0.00	£0.00	£0.00
Miscellaneous	£0.00	£0.00	£0.00	£0.00	£0.00	£0.00	£0.00	£0.00	£0.00	£0.00	£0.00	£0.00
TOTALS	£60,406.59	£5,033.88	£5,033.88	£5,033.88	£5,033.88	£5,033.88	£5,033.88	£5,033.88	£5,033.88	£5,033.88	£5,033.88	£5,033.88

The Bank interest paid is based on £450,000.00 capital at 11.5% per annum.

Allen Mbengeranwa

Profit and Loss Year One Summary Sheet

Papa Bengie's Bangor - Profit and loss Year One Summary Sheet

	Jan	Feb	Mar	Apr	May	Jun	Jul	Aug	Sep	Oct	Nov	December	Total
Sales													
Restaurant sales	£14,000.00	£14,000.00	£14,000.00	£14,000.00	£14,000.00	£14,000.00	£15,000.00	£15,000.00	£15,000.00	£15,000.00	£14,000.00	£15,000.00	£159,000.00
Catering	£0.00	£0.00	£0.00	£0.00	£0.00	£0.00	£0.00	£0.00	£0.00	£0.00	£0.00	£0.00	£0.00
Interest rebate	£0.00	£0.00	£2,352.01	£2,352.01	£2,352.01	£2,352.01	£2,352.01	£2,352.01	£2,352.01	£2,352.01	£2,352.01	£2,352.01	£23,520.10
Totals	£14,000.00	£14,000.00	£16,352.01	£16,352.01	£16,352.01	£16,352.01	£17,352.01	£17,352.01	£17,352.01	£16,352.01	£16,352.01	£17,352.01	£192,520.10
Cost of goods sold	£0.00	£1,000.00	£800.00	£800.00	£800.00	£800.00	£800.00	£900.00	£800.00	£800.00	£800.00	£900.00	£9,000.00
Gross Profit	£13,000.00	£13,000.00	£15,552.01	£15,552.01	£15,552.01	£15,552.01	£16,552.01	£16,552.01	£16,552.01	£16,552.01	£15,552.01	£16,552.01	£173,520.10
Overheads													
Sales Costs	£300.00	£300.00	£300.00	£300.00	£300.00	£300.00	£300.00	£300.00	£300.00	£300.00	£300.00	£300.00	£3,600.00
Admin Costs	£3,865.25	£3,865.25	£3,865.25	£3,865.25	£3,865.25	£3,865.25	£3,865.25	£3,865.25	£3,865.25	£3,865.25	£3,865.25	£3,865.25	£46,383.00
Establishment Costs	£3,383.72	£3,383.72	£3,383.72	£3,383.72	£3,383.72	£3,383.72	£3,383.72	£3,383.72	£3,383.72	£3,383.72	£3,383.72	£3,383.72	£40,604.64
Finance Costs	£5,033.88	£5,033.88	£5,033.88	£5,033.88	£5,033.88	£5,033.88	£5,033.88	£5,033.88	£5,033.88	£5,033.88	£5,033.88	£5,033.88	£60,406.56
Totals	£17,582.85	£17,582.85	£17,582.85	£17,582.85	£17,582.85	£17,582.85	£17,582.85	£17,582.85	£17,582.85	£17,582.85	£17,582.85	£17,582.85	£210,994.20
Net Profit/Loss	-£17,582.85	-£4,582.85	-£2,030.84	-£2,030.84	-£2,030.84	-£2,030.84	-£1,030.84	-£1,030.84	-£1,030.84	-£1,030.84	-£2,030.84	-£1,030.84	-£37,474.10
Cumulative	-£17,582.85	-£22,165.70	-£24,196.54	-£26,227.38	-£28,258.22	-£30,289.06	-£31,319.90	-£32,350.74	-£33,381.58	-£34,412.42	-£36,443.26	-£37,474.10	

Profit and Loss Year Two Summary Sheet

Papa Bengie's Bangor - Profit and loss year Two Summary Sheet

	Jan	Feb	Mar	Apr	May	Jun	Jul	Aug	Sep	Oct	Nov	Dec	Total
Sales													
Restaurant sales	£15,400.00	£15,400.00	£15,400.00	£15,400.00	£15,400.00	£15,400.00	£16,500.00	£16,500.00	£16,500.00	£16,500.00	£15,400.00	£16,500.00	£190,300.00
catering and delivery	£500.00	£500.00	£500.00	£500.00	£500.00	£500.00	£1,000.00	£500.00	£500.00	£500.00	£500.00	£2,000.00	£8,000.00
Interest rebate	£1,725.00	£1,725.00	£1,725.00	£1,725.00	£1,725.00	£1,725.00	£1,725.00	£1,725.00	£1,725.00	£1,725.00	£1,725.00	£1,725.00	£20,700.00
Totals	£17,625.00	£17,625.00	£17,625.00	£17,625.00	£17,625.00	£17,625.00	£19,225.00	£18,725.00	£18,725.00	£18,725.00	£17,625.00	£20,225.00	£219,000.00
cost of goods sold	£1,000.00	£1,000.00	£1,000.00	£1,000.00	£1,000.00	£1,000.00	£1,000.00	£1,000.00	£1,000.00	£1,000.00	£1,000.00	£1,000.00	£12,000.00
Gross Profit	£16,625.00	£16,725.00	£16,625.00	£16,625.00	£16,625.00	£16,625.00	£17,725.00	£18,225.00	£18,225.00	£17,725.00	£16,625.00	£19,225.00	£207,000.00
Overheads													
Sales Costs	£300.00	£300.00	£300.00	£300.00	£300.00	£300.00	£300.00	£300.00	£300.00	£300.00	£300.00	£300.00	£3,600.00
Admin Costs	£3,865.25	£3,865.25	£3,865.25	£3,865.25	£3,865.25	£3,865.25	£3,865.25	£3,865.25	£3,865.25	£3,865.25	£3,865.25	£3,865.25	£46,383.00
Establishment Costs	£8,701.90	£8,701.90	£8,701.90	£8,701.90	£8,701.90	£8,701.90	£8,701.90	£8,701.90	£8,701.90	£8,701.90	£8,701.90	£8,701.90	£104,422.80
Finance Costs	£4,171.38	£4,171.38	£4,171.38	£4,171.38	£4,171.38	£4,171.38	£4,171.38	£4,171.38	£4,171.38	£4,171.38	£4,171.38	£4,171.38	£50,056.56
Totals	£17,038.53	£17,038.53	£17,038.53	£17,038.53	£17,038.53	£17,038.53	£17,038.53	£17,038.53	£17,038.53	£17,038.53	£17,038.53	£17,038.53	£204,462.36
Net Profit/Loss	-£413.53	-£313.53	-£413.53	-£413.53	-£413.53	-£413.53	£1,186.47	£686.47	£1,186.47	£666.47	-£413.53	£2,186.47	£3,137.64
Cumulative	-£413.53	-£727.06	-£1,140.59	-£1,554.12	-£1,967.65	-£2,381.18	-£1,194.71	-£508.24	£678.23	£1,364.70	£951.17	£3,137.64	

Allen Mbengeranwa

Opening Stock Format

Item	Quantity	Unit	Retail	Total Cost	Total Revenue
Sauces:					
Sun dried tomato and herb					
Thai green curry sauce 10958	2-2.25		£16.51		£16.51
Caribbean spices			£20.00		£20.00
Sweet hickory barbeque sauce 47024	2-2.25 ltr		£14.00		£14.00
Red pepper and olive sauce 08552	2-2.25ltr		£17.58		£17.58
Vietnamese sweet chilli sauce 01327	2-2.35		£16.51		£16.51
Meats					
Beef Mince meat 01818	2.5kg	£3.78/kg			£9.45
Lamb mince meet	2.5kg	£5.74/kg			£14.35
Full chicken to produce 2 chicken breasts and 2 thighs	1.4kg	£3.35 each			£3.35
Bacon slices 26116	2-1.36	£5.58/kg			£15.19
BBQ chicken wings 12645	2.5kg	16p			£14.09
Tuna Supreme 140-170g	10	£1.33			£13.25
King Prawn Brochettes 50g	12	£1.00			£11.95
Vegetarian					
Veggie burger vegemince	24	46			£10.99
Accompaniments					
Skin on Potato wedges	2.5kg	1p			£2.69
Breaded mushrooms	1kg	5p			£3.79
Vegetable nuggets	2kg	6p			£7.09
Sesame seed buns 70293 10cm	48	13p			£6.29
French fries 71274 9/16"	6-2.5kg	72p kg			£10.75
Lettuce for shredding					
Hearts of romaine		59p			£1.17
Whole fresh tomatoes for slicing					
White onions					
Red onions					
Anchovy fillets in olive oil	25-50g	55p each			£13.95
Mayonnaise 40890	1-5ltr				£7.94
Olive oil					
Croutons					
Hard cheese					
Bleu cheese					
Pickles - sliced					
Mustard	2.27ltr				£9.47
Easy cook rice 28548	1-5 kg	£8.43			£8.43
Mustard 02873	2-2.27 ltr	£9.47			
Pita bread	36	13p			£4.65
Salsa	1kg				£5.15
Coleslaw Premiun	1-2kg	£3.99			£3.99
Chopped parsely					
Burger sauces - BBQ sauce					
Ranch dressing					
Honey and mustard 17216	6-1ltr				£23.07
Bleu cheese dressing 32161	2-2.5ltr				£14.44
Salt - LoSalt	2-6kg	£3.66			£7.31
Black Pepper (ground)	6-600g	£4.76			£28.56
Lemon juice	12-500ml	87p			£10.43
Sweet hickory BBQ sauce					
Ranch dressing					
Honey and mustard					
Bleu cheese dressing					
Bottled drinks					
Orange juice 55	24-275ml	43p			£10.28
Apple Juice	24-275ml	43p			£10.28
Rasberry and cranberry	24-275ml	43p			£10.28
Mineral water	23-330ml	26p			£6.03
BIB post mix					
Diet pepsi					£40.40
Tango orange					£40.40
7 up					£40.40

Pre Trading Cash Flow Forecast

Papa Benige's Bangor - Pre Trading Cash Flow Forcast				
	Period:			
	1	**2**	**3**	**TOTAL**
Cash Inflows				
Capital Intorduced	£0.00			£0.00
Grants	£0.00	£0.00	£0.00	£0.00
Loans	£428,728.95			£428,728.95
Total Inflows	£428,728.95	£0.00	£0.00	£428,728.95
Cash Outflows				
Premises	£375,000.00			£375,000.00
fixtures and fittings		£10,498.06		£10,498.06
equipment purchases			£32,690.89	£32,690.89
Start-Up costs	£10,540.00			£10,540.00
Total outflows	£385,540.00	£10,498.06	£32,690.89	£428,728.95
Outflows/Inflows	£43,188.95	-£10,498.06	-£32,690.89	£0.00
Balance brought forward		£43,188.95	£32,690.89	£0.00
Balance carried forward	£43,188.95	£32,690.89	£0.00	

Allen Mbengeranwa

Sales Costs

Papa Bengie's Bangor		Jan	Feb	Mar	Apr	May	Jun	Jul	Aug	Sep	Oct	Nov	Dec
Travel	0	0	0	0	0	0	0	0	0	0	0	0	0
Expenses	0	0	0	0	0	0	0	0	0	0	0	0	0
Entertainment	0	0	0	0	0	0	0	0	0	0	0	0	0
Christmas and 1/4 ly meetings				0			0			0			0
Advertising/PR	3600	300	300	300	300	300	300	300	300	300	300	300	300
Seminars	0						0			0			0
Shipping Insurance	0	0	0	0	0	0	0	0	0	0	0	0	0
Insurance Broker	0	0	0	0	0	0	0	0	0	0	0	0	0
Commission	0	0	0	0	0	0	0	0	0	0	0	0	0
Miscellaneous	3600	300	300	300	300	300	300	300	300	300	300	300	300
TOTALS	3600	300	300	300	300	300	300	300	300	300	300	300	300

Cash-flow forecasts – Year One

Papa Bengie's Bangor Cash Flow Sheet - YEAR ONE

	January	February	March	April	May	June	July	August	September	October	November	December	Total
Projected Sales	0	14,000	14,000	14,000	14,000	14,000	15,000	15,000	15,000	15,000	14,000	15,000	169,000
Cash Receipts (Cash in)													
Sales Invoiced	0	14,000	14,000	14,000	14,000	14,000	15,000	15,000	15,000	15,000	14,000	15,000	159,000
Catering													0
Interest rebate		2,352	2,352	2,352	2,352	2,352	2,352	2,352	2,352	2,352	2,352	2,352	23,523
Loan Proceeds	450,000												450,000
Total Cash In	450,000	14,000	16,352	16,352	16,352	16,352	17,352	17,352	17,352	17,352	16,352	17,352	632,523
Cash Disbursments (Cash out)													
Purchases (direct expenses)	0	1,000	800	800	800	800	800	800	800	800	800	800	9,000
Advertising	300	300	300	300	300	300	300	300	300	300	300	300	3,600
Cars incl Insurance)	100	100	100	100	100	100	100	100	100	100	100	100	1,200
Loan Interest		4,706	4,705	4,705	4,705	4,705	4,705	4,705	4,705	4,705	4,705	4,705	51,750
Insurance (Business Liability)	83	83	83	83	83	83	83	83	83	83	83	83	1,000
Professional Fees (Accounting & Legal)	2,000												2,000
Rent (Premises) + Rates	940	940	940	940	940	940	940	940	940	940	0	940	11,283
Telephone and fax		40		40		40		40		40		40	160
Utilities	500	500	500	500	500	500	500	500	500	500	500	500	6,000
Marketing/PR	300	300	300	300	300	300	300	300	300	300	300	300	3,600
Wages (Employees & payroll deductions	0	3,491	3,491	3,491	3,491	3,491	3,491	3,491	3,491	3,491	3,491	3,491	38,403
Loan Payments (capital NOT interest)		7,182	7,182	7,182	7,182	7,182	7,182	7,182	7,182	7,182	7,182	7,182	79,000
Purchase Fixed Assets	419788.95												419,789
Office Supplies & Expenses	50	50	50	50	50	50	50	50	50	50	50	50	600
Total Cash Out	424,063	18,651	18,491	18,451	18,451	18,491	18,451	18,451	18,491	18,451	18,451	18,491	627,384
Cash Flow Summary													
Opening Balance	0	25,937	21,296	19,148	17,049	14,950	12,811	11,712	10,614	9,475	8,376	6,277	
Add: Cash In	450,000	14,000	16,352	16,352	16,352	16,352	17,352	17,352	17,352	17,352	16,352	17,352	632,523
Subtract: Cash Out	424,063	18,651	18,491	18,451	18,451	18,491	18,451	18,451	18,491	18,451	18,451	18,491	627,384
Surplus or (Deficit)	25,937	-4,651	-2,139	-2,099	-2,099	-2,139	-1,099	-1,099	-1,139	-1,099	-2,099	-1,139	5,138
Closing Cash Balance	25,937	21,296	19,148	17,049	14,950	12,811	11,712	10,614	9,475	8,376	6,277	5,138	5,138

Cash flow assumptions:

An interest rebate of 50% is assumed to be recieved the following month

Loan repayements are assumed at £90,000.00 per 12 months but over the first 11 months in the first year only £79,000.00

Sales are assumed as 500 per week with an average spending of £7

Average Direct cost per meal £1.50

Allen Mbengeranwa

Cash-flow forecasts – Year Two

Papa Bengie's Bangor Cash Flow Sheet - YEAR TWO

	January	February	March	April	May	June	July	August	September	October	November	December	Total
Projected Sales	16,400	16,400	16,400	16,400	16,400	16,400	16,500	16,500	16,500	16,500	16,400	16,500	190,300
Cash Receipts (Cash in)													
Sales Invoiced	15,400	15,400	15,400	15,400	15,400	15,400	16,500	16,500	16,500	16,500	15,400	16,500	190,300
Catering and delivery	500	600	500	500	500	1,000	500	500	500	500	2,000	2,000	8,600
Interest rebate	1,725	1,725	1,725	1,725	1,725	1,725	1,725	1,725	1,725	1,725	1,725	1,725	20,700
Total Cash In	17,625	17,725	17,625	17,625	17,625	17,625	19,225	18,725	19,225	18,725	17,625	20,225	219,600
Cash Disbursements (Cash out)													
Purchases (direct expenses)	1,000	1,000	1,000	1,000	1,000	1,000	1,000	1,000	1,000	1,000	1,000	1,000	12,000
Advertising	300	300	300	300	300	300	300	300	300	300	300	300	3,600
Cars incl. Insurance	100	100	100	100	100	100	100	100	100	100	100	100	1,200
Loan Interest	3,450	3,450	3,450	3,450	3,450	3,450	3,450	3,450	3,450	3,450	3,450	3,450	41,400
Insurance (Business Liability)	83	83	83	83	83	83	83	83	83	83	83	83	1,000
Professional Fees (Accounting & Legal)	500												500
Rent (Premises) + Rates	940	940	940	940	940	940	940	940	940	940	940		11,283
Telephone and fax	40	40	40	40	40	40	40	40	40	40	40	40	160
Utilities	500	500	500	500	500	500	500	500	500	500	500	500	6,000
Marketing	300	300	300	300	300	300	300	300	300	300	300	300	3,600
Wages (Employees & payroll deductions)	3,491	3,491	3,491	3,491	3,491	3,491	3,491	3,491	3,491	3,491	3,491	3,491	41,894
Loan Payments (capital NOT interest)	7,500	7,500	7,500	7,500	7,500	7,500	7,500	7,500	7,500	7,500	7,500	7,500	90,000
Office Supplies & Expenses	50	50	50	50	50	50	50	50	50	50	50	50	600
Total Cash Out	18,215	17,715	17,755	17,715	17,716	17,755	17,715	17,715	17,755	17,716	17,715	17,755	213,237
Cash Flow Summary													
Opening Balance	5,138	4,548	4,559	4,429	4,339	4,249	4,120	5,630	6,640	8,111	9,121	9,031	
Add: Cash In	17,625	17,725	17,625	17,625	17,625	17,625	19,225	18,725	19,225	18,725	17,625	20,225	219,600
Subtract: Cash Out	18,215	17,715	17,755	17,715	17,716	17,755	17,715	17,715	17,755	17,716	17,715	17,755	213,237
Surplus or (Deficit)	-590	10	-130	-90	-90	-130	1,510	1,010	1,470	1,010	-90	2,470	6,363
Closing Cash Balance	4,548	4,559	4,429	4,339	4,249	4,120	5,630	6,640	8,111	9,121	9,031	11,501	11,501

Cash flow assumptions:

An interest rebate of 50% is assumed to be recieved the following month

Loan repayments are assumed at £90,000.00 per 12 months with balance at the end of year 1 at £360,000.00

Sales are assumed as 500 per week with an average spending of £7

Average Direct cost per meal £1.50

The is an estimated increase of 10% of sales in the second year.

July and September catering figures are University led with graduation and freshers week

December catering figures are based on Chirstmas sales and parties.

24088193R00056

Printed in Great Britain
by Amazon